SOUPS

Cook Books from Amish Kitchens

Phyllis Pellman Good • Rachel Thomas Pellman

Good Books

Intercourse, PA 17534

SOUPS

Cook Books from Amish Kitchens

A bowl of homemade soup can warm any occasion. Rich yet simple, filling yet not fattening, this is basic, sturdy fare.

We've selected the favorites (complete with rivels), from Old Time Beef Stew to Cold Bread Soup. Try your own additions to these and make them yours!

Cover art and design by Cheryl A. Benner.
Design and art in body by Craig N. Heisey; calligraphy by Gayle Smoker.
This special edition is an adaptation of *Soups: From Amish and Mennonite Kitchens, Pennsylvania Dutch Cookbooks,* and from *Cook Books by Good Books.* Copyright © 1982, 1991, 1996 by Good Books, Intercourse, PA 17534. ISBN: 1-56148-194-7. All rights reserved. Printed in the United States of America.

Contents

Chicken Corn Rivel Soup

3-4 lb. stewing chicken Makes 8-10 servings
2 Tbsp. salt
¼ tsp. pepper
1½ cups celery, chopped
1 medium onion, chopped
2 Tbsp. minced parsley
1 quart corn (fresh, frozen, or canned)
Rivels

1. In large kettle cover chicken with water. Add salt and pepper. Cook until soft. Remove bones and skin from chicken and cut meat into small pieces.
2. Heat broth to boiling point and add remaining ingredients. Cook about 15 minutes. Add meat. Heat thoroughly. Garnish with hard-boiled egg or parsley.

Rivels

1 cup flour
1 egg
¼ cup milk

1. Combine flour and egg. Add milk.

Mix rivels by cutting with two forks to make crumbs the size of cherry stones. Drop rivels into boiling broth while stirring to prevent rivels from packing together.

Chicken Rice Soup

Makes 6 servings

1 whole chicken, cut apart
2 quarts water
1 onion, chopped
¾ cup celery, chopped
1½ tsp. salt
dash pepper
1 cup rice, cooked

1. In a large kettle combine chicken, water, onion, celery, salt, and pepper. Cook until chicken is tender, about 1½ hours.
2. Remove chicken from broth and pick meat from bone. Return to broth with rice. Heat thoroughly.

Vegetable Soup

1 beef soup bone   Makes 8 servings
2 quarts water
1 tsp. salt
1 cup carrots, diced
½ cup celery, diced
1 quart tomatoes or tomato juice
1 small onion, chopped
2 quarts mixed vegetables
1½ cups potatoes, diced
1½ cups cabbage, thinly sliced
1 cup macaroni
½ cup rice

1. Cook soup bone with salt in 2 quarts water until soft. Remove from broth and cool enough so meat can be taken from bone and cut into small pieces. Return meat to broth.
2. Add all other ingredients plus water enough to cover. Cook until vegetables are tender, about 20 minutes. Add additional salt and pepper to taste.

Any vegetable in season can be used – corn, peas, lima beans, yellow beans, etc.

Chilly Day Soup

1 large carrot   Makes 6-8 servings
2 cups water
2 large onions
1 quart diced potatoes
2 Tbsp. rice
⅓ cup macaroni
1 tsp. salt
¼ tsp. pepper
2 cups milk
2 Tbsp. butter

1. Chop carrot and cook in 2 cups water. While cooking chop onions.
2. When carrot is partially cooked add onions, potatoes, rice, macaroni, salt, and pepper. Add enough water to cover and cook until tender.
3. Add milk and butter and heat thoroughly.

Variations:
     1. Add 2 cups chicken broth in place of milk and butter.
     2. Add 1 cup cooked meat to soup when milk is added.

Old Time Beef Stew

2 lbs. beef cubes   Makes 6 servings
2 Tbsp. shortening
1 large onion, sliced
4 cups boiling water or tomato juice
1 Tbsp. salt
1 Tbsp. lemon juice
1 Tbsp. sugar
1 Tbsp. worcestershire sauce
½ Tbsp. pepper
½ Tbsp. paprika
dash of allspice or ground cloves
6 carrots cut in quarters
6 potatoes cut in chunks
½ cup cold water
¼ cup flour

1. Brown beef cubes in shortening for about 20 minutes. Add onion, water, salt, lemon juice, sugar, worcestershire sauce, pepper, paprika, and allspice or cloves. Cover and simmer 2 hours. Stir occasionally to prevent sticking.
2. Add vegetables. Simmer 30 minutes longer.
3. Combine water and flour. Stir until smooth. Pull vegetables and meat to one side of pan. Add flour mixture and

stir until gravy is thickened.

Variation:
   Add 1½ cups green beans with vegetables.

Delicious Vegetable Soup
   2 Tbsp. butter   Makes 4-6 servings
   1 onion, chopped
   1 lb. hamburger
   1½ tsp. salt
   1 cup carrots, diced
   ½ cup celery, chopped
   1 cup potatoes, diced
   2 cups tomato juice
   2 cups milk
   ¼ cup flour

1. Brown meat and onion in butter. Add remaining ingredients except milk and flour and cook until vegetables are tender.
2. Combine milk and flour and stir until smooth. Add to soup and cook until thickened.

Beef or Chicken Noodle Soup

Beef soup bone or   Makes 6 servings
    boney chicken parts
1 celery stalk, chopped
1 onion, chopped
½ lb. noodles
salt and pepper

1. Cook beef or chicken with onion and celery in 3 quarts water until meat is tender. Remove meat from broth and pick from bones.
2. Add noodles to boiling broth and cook until tender. Return meat to soup. Salt and pepper to taste.

Ham Noodle Soup

1 ham bone   Makes 6 servings
1 Tbsp. onion, chopped
1 celery stalk, chopped
½ lb. noodles
salt and pepper

1. Cook ham bone, onion, and celery in 3 quarts of water until meat is tender.

Remove meat from broth and pick from bone.
2. Add noodles to boiling broth and cook until tender. Return meat to soup. Salt and pepper to taste.

Chili Con Carne

2 Tbsp. shortening   Makes 6 servings
1 onion, diced
1 clove garlic (optional)
1 lb. ground beef
1½ tsp. salt
1 Tbsp. flour
2½ tsp. chili powder
2 cups tomatoes
1 cup hot water
3 cups cooked kidney beans

1. Melt shortening and sauté onion and garlic. Add hamburger. Brown meat and sprinkle with salt, flour, and chili powder.
2. Add tomatoes and hot water. Cover and simmer for 1 hour.
3. Add kidney beans and heat thoroughly.

Creamy Potato Soup

3 Tbsp. butter   Makes 4-6 servings
1 onion, diced
4 large potatoes, cubed
3 Tbsp. parsley, chopped
3 stalks celery and leaves, chopped
2 large carrots, chopped or grated
2 tsp. salt
¼ tsp. paprika
1½ cups boiling water
White sauce

1. Sauté onion in butter until tender. Add remaining ingredients except white sauce and cook until vegetables are tender.
2. Add white sauce and stir until blended.

White Sauce

4 cups milk
2 Tbsp. flour
4 Tbsp. butter
2 chicken bouillon cubes
1 tsp. salt
¼ tsp. pepper

1. Mix ½ cup milk with flour. Heat

remaining milk to boiling. Add flour mixture and stir constantly until thickened. Add remaining ingredients and stir until bouillon cubes are dissolved.

Potato Soup with Rivels

¼ cup butter   Makes 5 servings
10-12 medium potatoes, peeled and diced
salt and pepper to taste
Rivels (see page 4 for directions)

1. In saucepan combine butter, potatoes, salt, and pepper. Cover with water. Bring to a boil. Add rivels. Cook until potatoes are tender. Sprinkle with parsley leaves before serving.

"You don't even need crackers with this!"

Potato Soup

¼ cup celery, diced   Makes 6-8 servings
3 cups water
2 cups potatoes, diced
1 medium onion, chopped
salt and pepper to taste
1 quart milk
2 Tbsp. butter
3 hard-boiled eggs, chopped

1. Boil celery in 1 cup of water. When partially soft add remaining water, potatoes, onion, salt, and pepper. Cook until tender.
2. Add milk and chopped eggs. Heat thoroughly. Add butter and serve.

Variations:
   1. When potatoes, onion, and celery are soft, put in blender with half of the milk which has been heated. Add ½ cup grated cheese and blend until smooth. Add remaining hot milk and butter and stir. Garnish with chopped or shredded hard-boiled eggs.
   2. Add 1 diced carrot to vegetables while cooking. Garnish with parsley flakes.

Potato Soup with Sausage Balls

2 Tbsp. margarine   Makes 4 servings
1 small onion, chopped
1 stalk celery, chopped
3 or 4 potatoes, diced
½ lb. loose pork sausage formed into
   small balls about 1" in diameter
2 tsp. salt
1½ cup water
1 egg
3 cups milk

1. Sauté onion and celery in butter. Add potatoes, sausage balls, salt, and water and cook until potatoes are tender.
2. Break egg into potato mixture and stir with fork until cooked.
3. Add milk and heat thoroughly.

Oyster and Potato Stew

2 medium potatoes, diced   Makes 4 servings
1 celery stalk, chopped
salt
1½ cups water
1½ dozen stewing oysters
¼ tsp. salt
3 cups milk
1 Tbsp. butter
pepper

1. Cook potatoes and celery in 1 cup of water until tender. Salt to taste.
2. In the remaining ½ cup water, cook the oysters with ¼ tsp. salt. Heat until boiling and the oysters begin to curl.
3. Add milk, butter, and vegetables. Heat thoroughly. Add pepper to taste.

Oyster Stew

1 quart milk   Makes 4 servings
1 pint stewing oysters
2 Tbsp. butter
1 tsp. pepper

1. In a 2 quart saucepan heat milk to the boiling point.
2. In a frying pan melt the butter and brown it.
3. Drain the oysters; then add them one at a time to the browned butter. Cook for only 2 to 3 minutes. Add the pepper.
4. Add the oysters and butter to the hot milk and serve at once.

"Don't overcook oysters – and you'll have tender meat and a flavorful broth."

Clam Stew

¼ cup butter or margarine   Makes 6 servings

1 medium onion, minced
½ cup celery, finely chopped
4 potatoes, diced
½ tsp. salt
2 cups water
12 clams or
   2 8 oz. cans of clams, chopped
3 Tbsp. flour
1 quart milk
3 hard boiled eggs, diced

1. Melt butter or margarine; sauté onion and celery until soft but not brown.
2. Add potatoes and salt. Cover with 2 cups water. Simmer until soft.
3. Add clams with their juices and cook an additional 10 minutes.
4. Stir in the flour. Gradually add milk and cook slowly until mixture thickens.
5. Stir in eggs just before serving.

Salmon Chowder

3-4 potatoes, diced   Makes 6 servings
2 Tbsp. onion, minced
2 Tbsp. celery, chopped
1 lb. canned salmon (remove skin and
    bones), flaked
1 cup corn
1 tsp. salt
pinch pepper
1 quart milk
2 Tbsp. butter

1. Combine potatoes, onion, and celery in saucepan. Add water enough to cover and cook until vegetables are tender.
2. Add salmon, corn, salt, pepper, and milk. Heat slowly. Add butter and serve with crackers.

"A simple, quick, and satisfying meal."

Rice Soup

    1 2 lb. beef soup   Makes 8-10 servings
       bone
    3 tsp. salt
    ¼ tsp. pepper
    2 quarts beef broth
    1 cup rice
    Rivels (see page 4 for directions)

1. Boil soup bone with salt and pepper in enough water to cover, until tender. Remove meat from bone and set aside. Measure broth and add water if needed to equal 2 quarts.
2. Add rice to broth and cook 15-20 minutes until rice is tender.
3. Add rivels to soup. Add meat. Boil slowly for about 7 minutes.

"We like it very much. It's quite hearty and suits my farmer husband quite well."

Corn Chowder

2 slices bacon   Makes 4-6 servings
¼ cup chopped onion
2 medium potatoes, cubed
2 cups corn
½ cup chopped celery
½ tsp. salt
¼ tsp. pepper
2 cups chicken broth
2 Tbsp. flour
2 cups milk

1. In 3-quart saucepan fry bacon until crisp. Remove and drain, reserving drippings. Crumble bacon and set aside.
2. Cook onions in bacon drippings until soft but not brown. Add potatoes, corn, celery, salt, pepper, and 1½ cups chicken broth. Bring to a boil. Reduce heat. Cover and simmer 15-20 minutes.
3. Blend flour and remaing chicken broth. Add to vegetable mixture. Cook and stir until slightly thickened and bubbly. Reduce heat.
4. Add milk. Heat thoroughly but do not boil. Top with crumbled bacon.

Celery Chowder

1 large onion, diced   Makes 4-6 servings
1 Tbsp. butter
3 cups green celery, chopped
1 cup potatoes, diced
4 cups milk
2 hard-boiled eggs, chopped
salt and pepper to taste

1. Sauté onion in butter until soft. Add celery and potatoes. Cover with water and cook until soft.
2. Add milk and eggs and heat thoroughly. Salt and pepper to taste.

Broccoli and Cauliflower Soup

2 cups broccoli   Makes 4 servings
2 cups cauliflower
½ cup water
1 tsp. salt
½ tsp. basil
2 Tbsp. butter
2½ Tbsp. flour
3 cups milk

1. In saucepan combine broccoli, cauliflower,

22

water, salt, and basil. Cook until tender.
2. In separate pan melt butter until
lightly browned. Add flour and stir until
smooth. Gradually add milk, stirring
constantly until thickened. Pour over
vegetable mixture and stir until blended.

Cream of Broccoli Soup

1¼ lb. broccoli   Makes 8 servings
4 Tbsp. butter
¼ cup mushrooms, chopped
1 Tbsp. onion, chopped
4 Tbsp. flour
3½ cups milk
1 lb. sharp cheddar cheese, grated
1 tsp. salt

1. Cook broccoli. Chop and set aside.
2. Melt butter in large, heavy pan. Add
mushrooms and onion. Sauté until tender.
3. Add flour and stir until bubbly.
4. Gradually add 1½ cups milk, stirring
constantly to prevent lumps. Add cheese
and stir until smooth. Add remaining
milk.
5. Add broccoli and heat thoroughly.

Ham and Cabbage Soup

2 Tbsp. butter or   Makes 6 servings
   margarine
¼ cup onion, minced
¼ cup celery, chopped
¼ cup flour
½ tsp. salt
⅛ tsp. pepper
3 cups water
2 cups cabbage, chopped or shredded
2 cups ham, cooked and diced
¾ cup dairy sour cream

1. Melt butter; then sauté onion and celery until tender. Add flour, salt, and pepper, blending till smooth.
2. Add water and cook until mixture comes to a boil, stirring constantly.
3. Add cabbage. Cover and simmer until cabbage is tender, about 10 minutes.
4. Stir in ham and cook until heated through.
5. Blend in sour cream. Heat, but do not boil.

Cream of Onion Soup

2 Tbsp. margarine   Makes 6 servings
4 Tbsp. flour
2 cups chicken stock
4 cups milk
4 Tbsp. margarine
1 cup onion, chopped
½ tsp. salt
¼ tsp. pepper
¼ cup parsley
4 Tbsp. cream

1. Melt 2 Tbsp. of margarine. Add flour and stir until smooth.
2. Add chicken stock, stirring constantly until smooth and thickened. Gradually add milk. Continue stirring until mixture comes to the boiling point, then set soup aside.
3. In a separate pan sauté onion in 4 Tbsp. of margarine. When tender add seasonings and cream. Simmer gently for 15 minutes.
4. Add onion mixture to soup. Heat but do not boil.

Tomato Soup

2 cups tomato juice Makes 4-6 servings
(home canned with peppers, onion, and
celery)
½ tsp. baking soda
1 quart milk
1 tsp. salt
dash of pepper
2 Tbsp. butter

1. Heat tomato juice to boiling. When boiling add baking soda and stir quickly because mixture will foam. Remove from heat.
2. Meanwhile, heat milk. Do not boil. Add salt, pepper, and butter. When milk is hot, add hot tomato mixture to it. Serve soup with crackers.

"We used to eat this with toasted cheese sandwiches for lunch. Now I like to serve it as an appetizer."

Bean Soup

2 cups dried navy beans   Makes 8 servings
1 ham bone
2 quarts water
salt and pepper
2 quarts milk
3 Tbsp. butter

1. Soak beans overnight in enough water to cover. In the morning, drain beans. Add water and ham bone. Cook slowly until meat and beans are soft. Pick meat from bone. Chop and return to bean mixture.
2. Add milk. Heat thoroughly. Season with salt and pepper to taste. Add butter and serve.

Variations:
1. Add ½ cup chopped onion.
2. Add ½ cup chopped celery.
3. Add ½ cup chopped carrot.

Pea Soup

1 quart peas   Makes 8 servings
   (fresh or frozen)
3 quarts milk
Rivels (see page 4 for directions)
1 tsp. pepper
6 hard-boiled eggs, sliced
¼ lb. butter

1. Cook peas until tender. In separate pan bring to boil 1 quart of milk.
2. Make rivels and drop by small amounts from the back of a spoon into the boiling milk. Boil 5-7 minutes.
3. Add remaining milk and salt. Add pepper, eggs, peas, and butter. Heat thoroughly.

"The rivels make this one stick to your ribs!"

Split Pea Soup

1 lb. dried split peas   Makes 6-8 servings
2 quarts water
1 ham hock
1 cup celery, finely chopped
1 medium onion, finely chopped
2 carrots, finely chopped or shredded
salt and pepper to taste

1. Combine peas and water. Bring to a boil and boil 2 minutes. Remove from heat. Cover and let set for 1 hour.
2. Add remaining ingredients. Bring to boiling point. Reduce heat and simmer 2½-3 hours until peas look creamed and ham hock is tender. Remove ham hock. Trim meat from bone and dice. Return meat to soup. Heat thoroughly and serve.

Additional water or milk may be added to soup for a thinner consistency.

Cold Bread Soup

Cut bread in chunks or cubes. Sugar to taste and pour cold milk over bread and sugar.

Huckleberries, cherries, or peaches in season can be added. Serve in large soup bowl.

Coffee Soup

Break 1 piece of bread into a cup. Fill cup with hot coffee: add sugar and cream to taste.

"These recipes probably came about during the Depression. But I still get hungry for a bowl of Coffee or Cold Bread Soup at breakfast or lunch!"

Stewed Crackers and Soft-Cooked Eggs

¼ - ½ lb. (about 50 or 60) buttermilk, saltine, or round soup crackers
2½ cups milk
2 Tbsp. butter or margarine
4 or 5 eggs

Makes 4-5 servings

1. Butter bottom and sides of a 1½ quart casserole. Lay dry crackers in casserole.
2. Heat milk to scalding. Pour over crackers. Cover casserole and let stand at least 5 minutes, checking once to make sure crackers are in the milk.
3. Just before serving, heat butter until browned and pour over crackers.
4. Cook the eggs separately (4 minutes in boiling water), and serve with the crackers, breaking an egg over each person's mound of crackers or along side.

Stewed Pretzels

pretzels
2 Tbsp. butter
1½ cups milk

1. Fill a covered 1½ quart dish about half full of broken pretzels. (Thicker pretzels are better than thin ones or pretzel sticks). Pour boiling water to level of pretzels. Let soak at least ½ hour. When pretzels are soft drain off any excess water.
2. Melt butter and allow it to brown. Add milk. Bring to boil. Pour hot milk over pretzels. Replace cover and allow to stand 5-10 minutes before serving.

"It's a good way to use stale pretzels!"